Partners in Praise

Hymns, Gospel Songs, and Seasonal Selections
Arranged for One Piano, Four Hands

by Marilynn Ham

with Meryl Ham

Student: Easy to Moderate
Teacher: Moderate to Advanced

Lillenas PUBLISHING COMPANY
Kansas City, MO 64141

CONTENTS

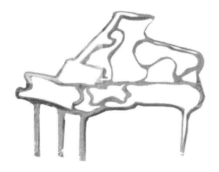

4

For the Beauty of the Earth

with Fairest Lord Jesus

SECONDO

Easy - Moderate

CONRAD KOCHER
Arranged by Marilynn Ham

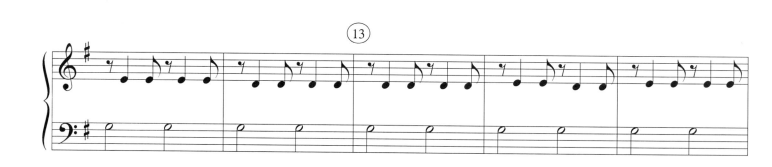

For the Beauty of the Earth

with Fairest Lord Jesus

PRIMO

CONRAD KOCHER
Arranged by Marilynn Ham

Moderate - Advanced

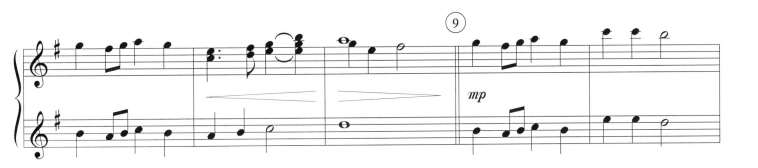

SECONDO

"Fairest Lord Jesus" (*Schlesische Volkslieder*)

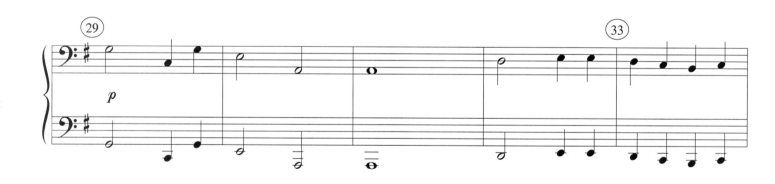

"Fairest Lord Jesus" (*Schlesische Volkslieder*)

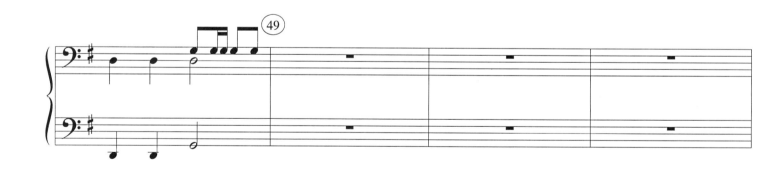

Cares Chorus

with Turn Your Eyes upon Jesus

SECONDO

Moderate - Advanced

KELLY WILLARD
Arranged by Marilynn Ham

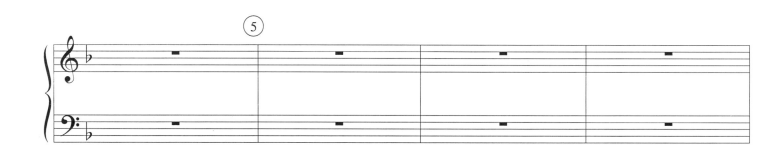

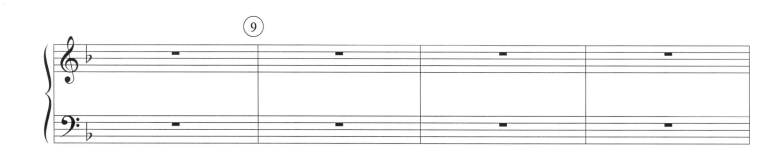

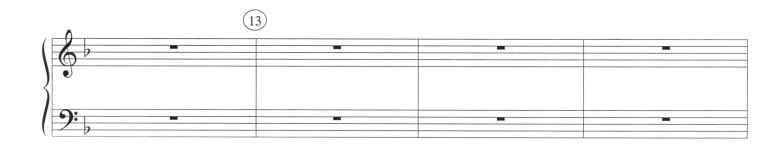

Cares Chorus

with Turn Your Eyes upon Jesus

KELLY WILLARD
Arranged by Marilynn Ham

PRIMO

Easy - Moderate

With pedal, but very clear

SECONDO

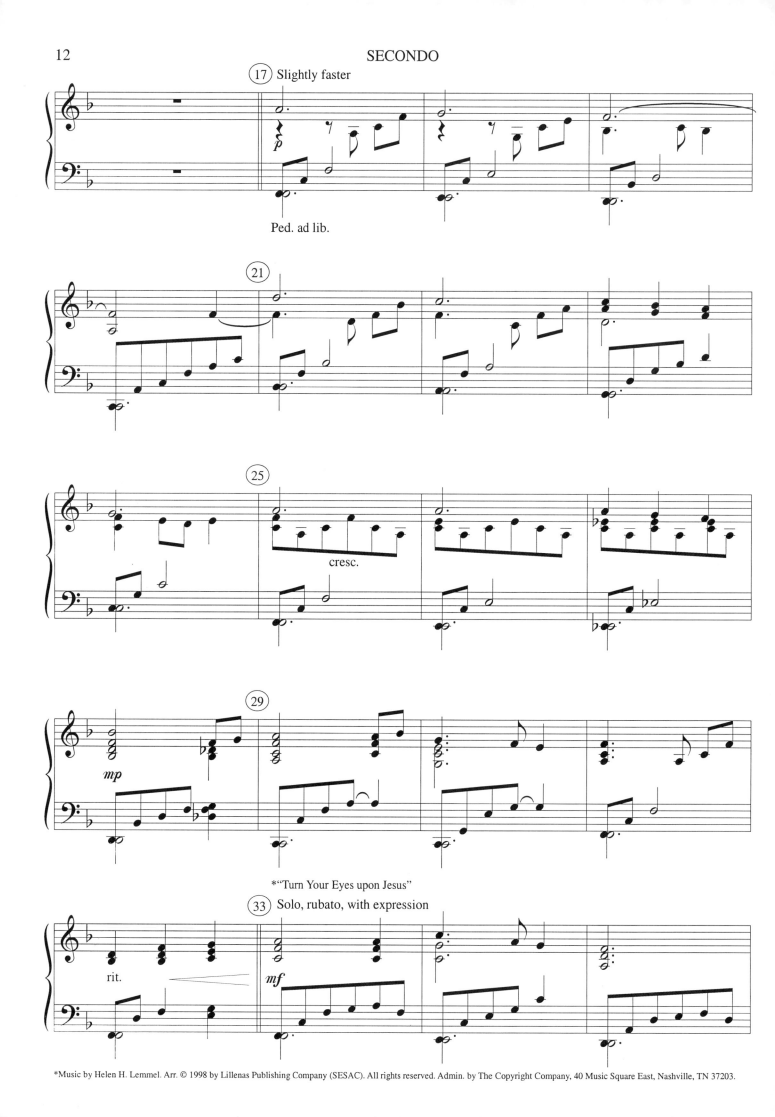

*"Turn Your Eyes upon Jesus"

*"Turn Your Eyes upon Jesus"

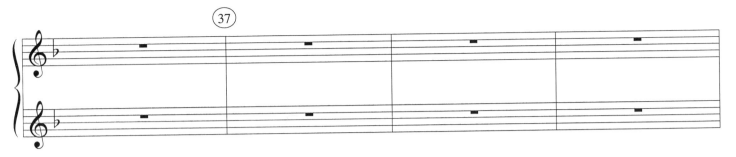

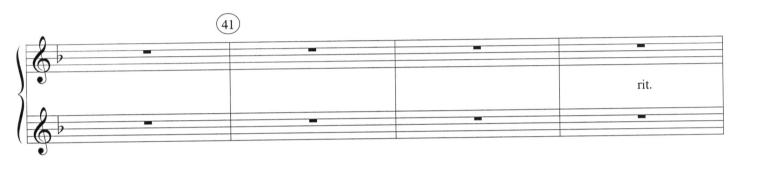

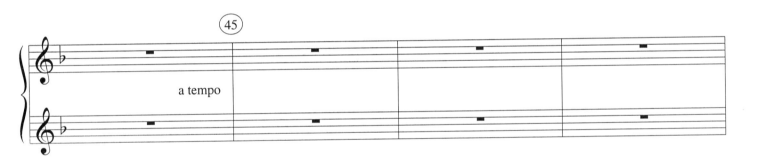

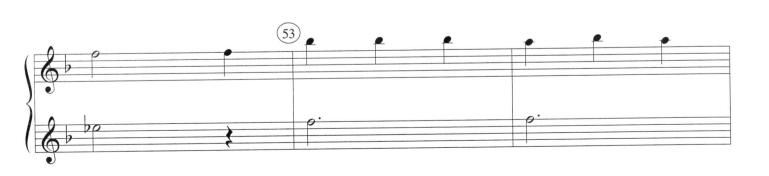

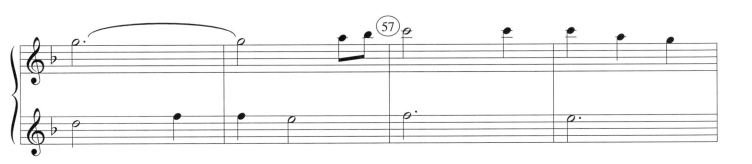

Guide Me, O Thou Great Jehovah

SECONDO
Moderate - Advanced

JOHN HUGHES
Arranged by Marilynn Ham

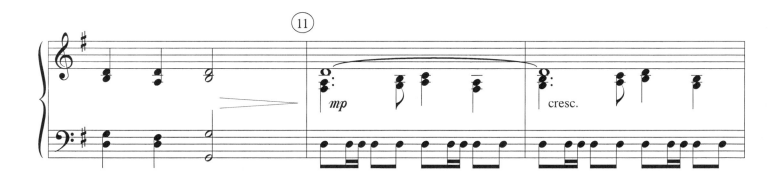

Guide Me, O Thou Great Jehovah

PRIMO
Easy - Moderate

JOHN HUGHES
Arranged by Marilynn Ham

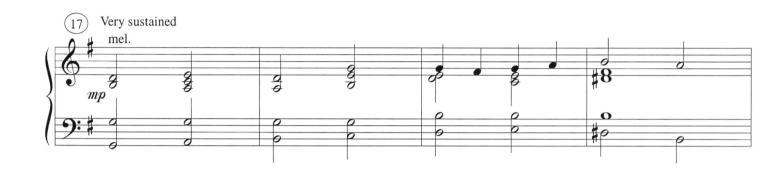

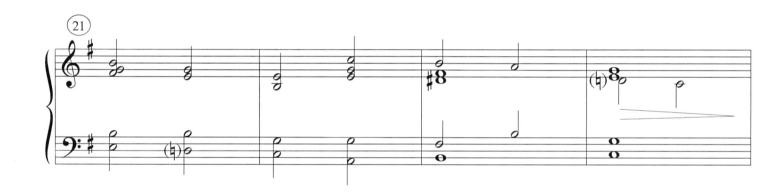

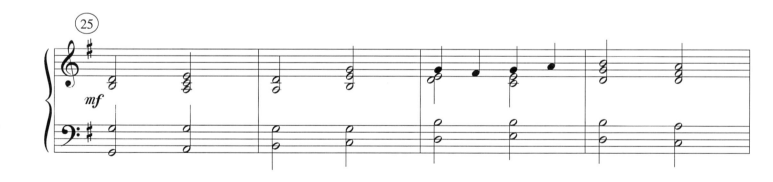

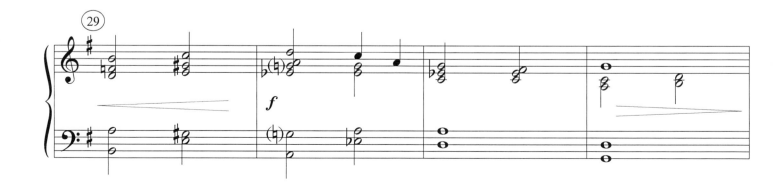

Very sustained

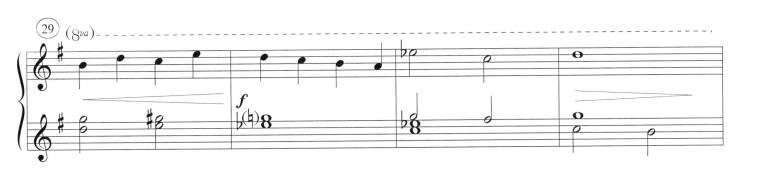

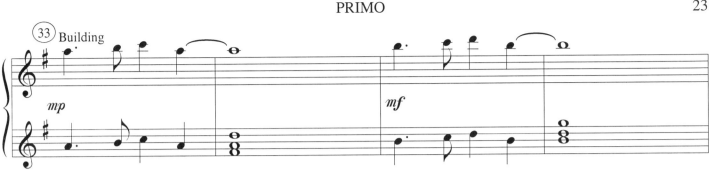

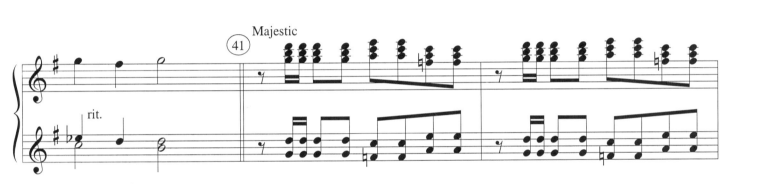

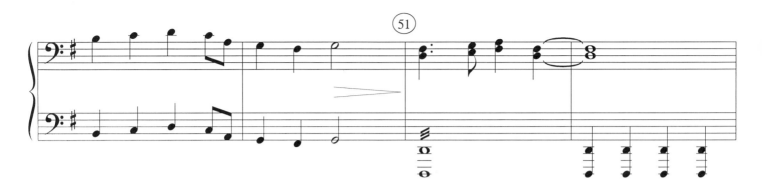

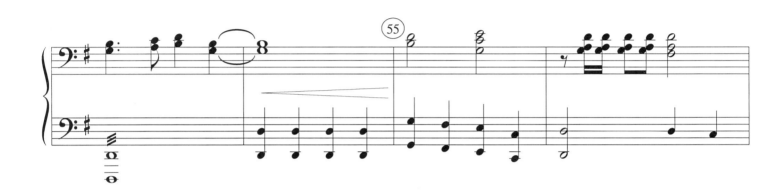

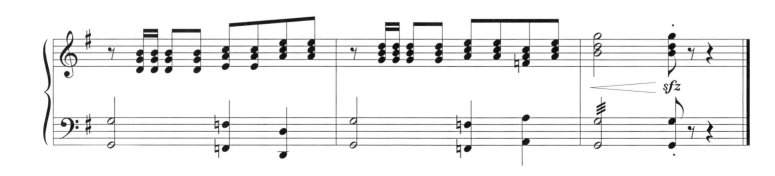

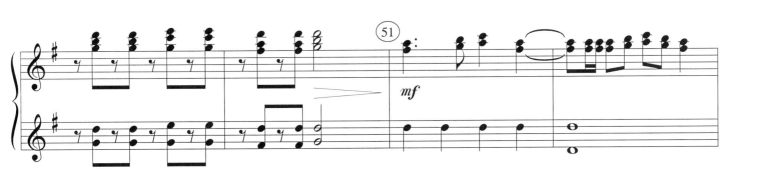

Get All Excited

with The King Is Coming

SECONDO

WILLIAM J. GAITHER
Arranged by Marilynn Ham

Moderate - Advanced

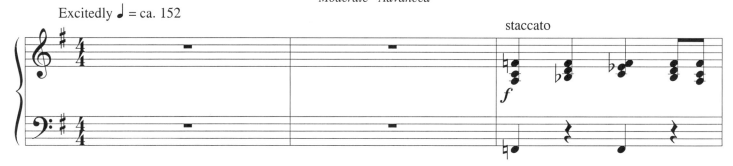

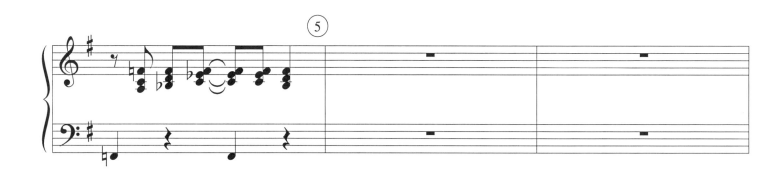

Get All Excited

with The King Is Coming

WILLIAM J. GAITHER
Arranged by Marilynn Ham

PRIMO
Easy - Moderate

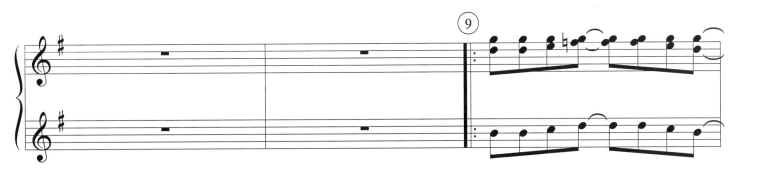

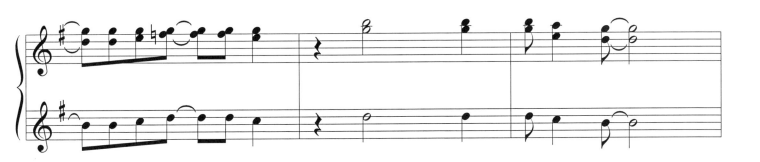

SECONDO

*"The King Is Coming"
Slower, tempo rubato

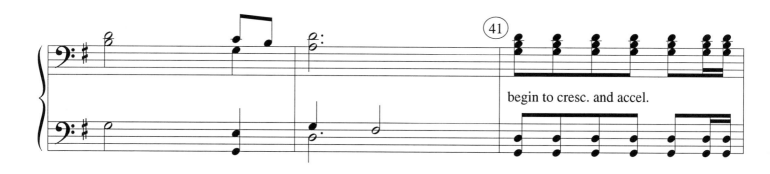

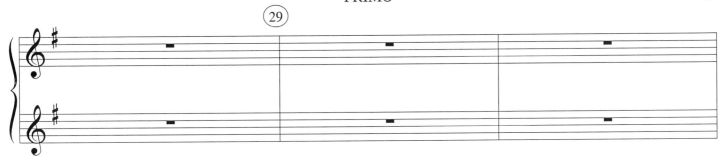

*"The King Is Coming"

Slower, tempo rubato

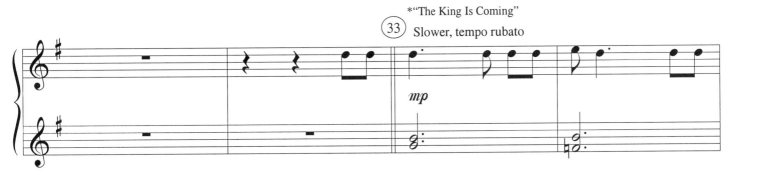

begin to cresc. and accel.

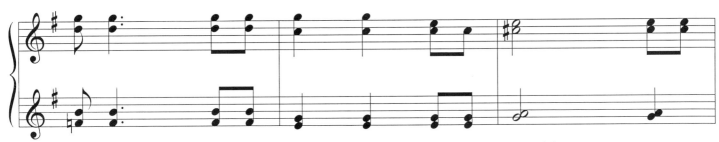

molto accel.

(63) Fast tempo, like beginning

sub. *p*

cresc.

(67)

f

(71)

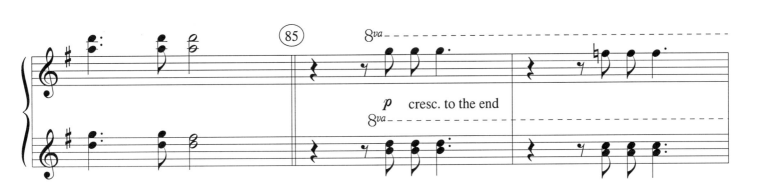

Angels We Have Heard on High

SECONDO
Moderate - Advanced

Traditional French Melody
Arranged by Marilynn and Meryl Ham

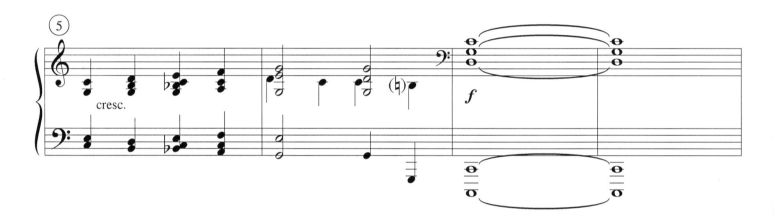

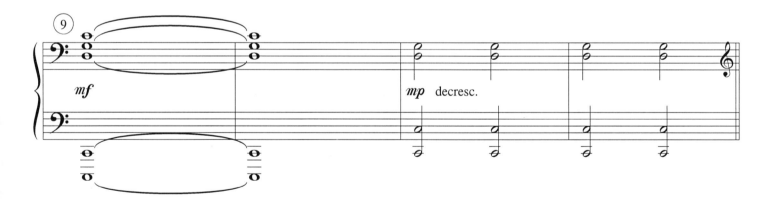

Ped. ad lib.

Angels We Have Heard on High

PRIMO
Easy - Moderate

Traditional French Melody
Arranged by Marilynn and Meryl Ham

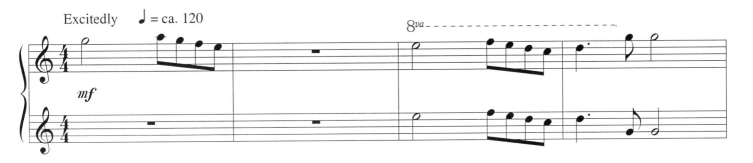

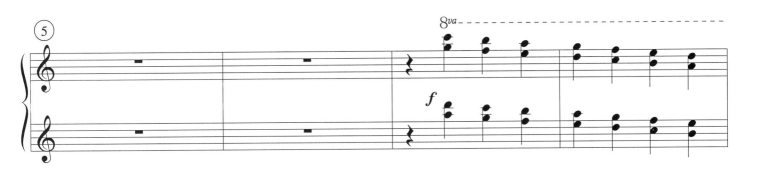

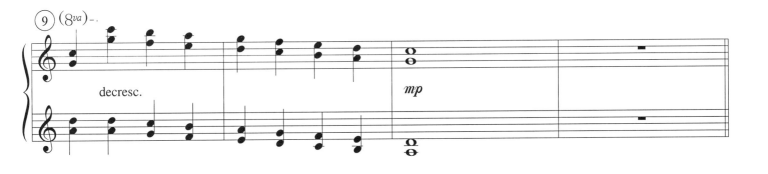

SECONDO

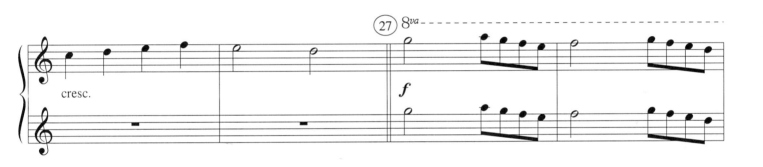

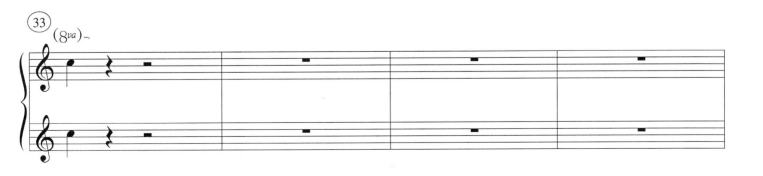

Ped. ad lib.

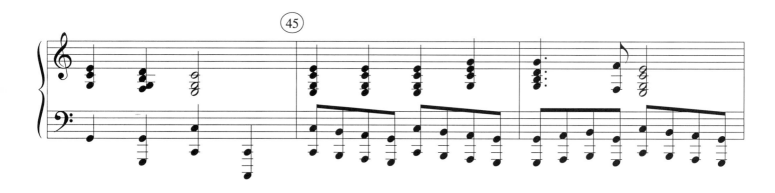

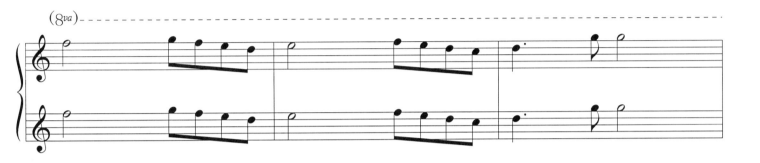

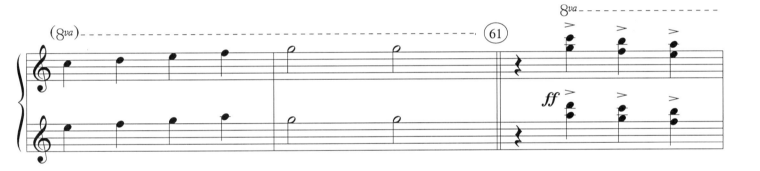

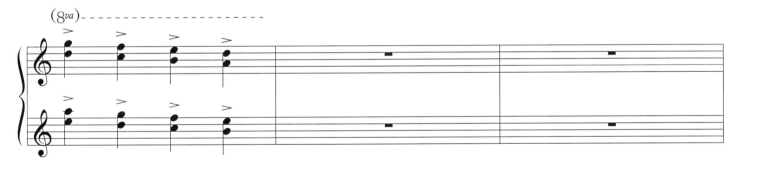

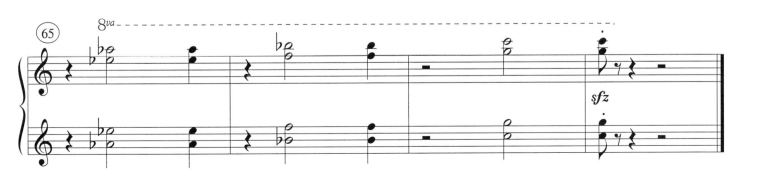

This Little Light of Mine

SECONDO

Moderate - Advanced

Traditional
Arranged by Marilynn and Meryl Ham

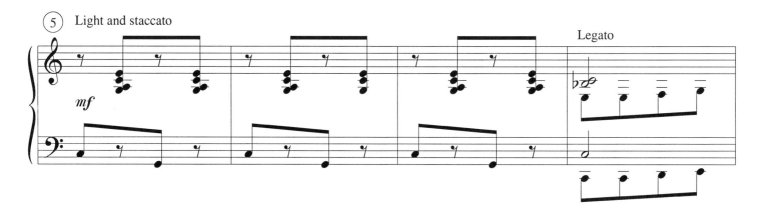

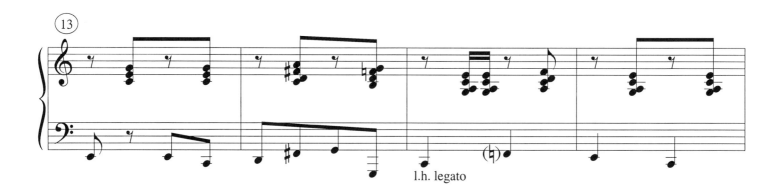

This Little Light of Mine

PRIMO
Easy - Moderate

Traditional
Arranged by Marilynn and Meryl Ham

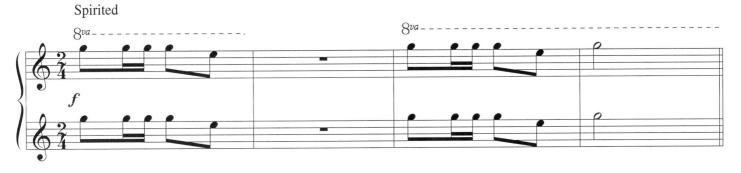

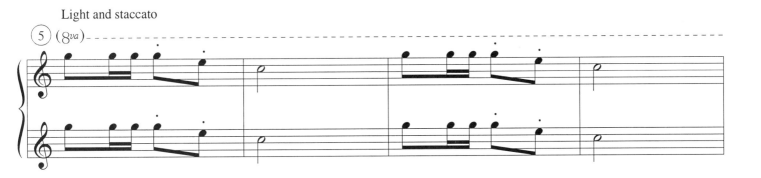

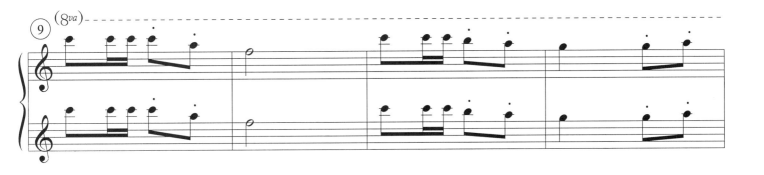

a tempo
mp

legato, no pedal

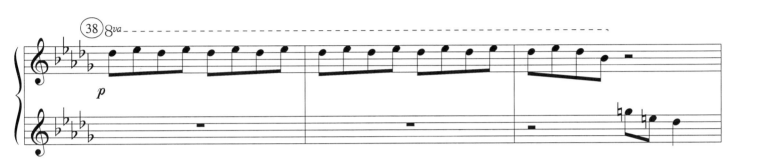
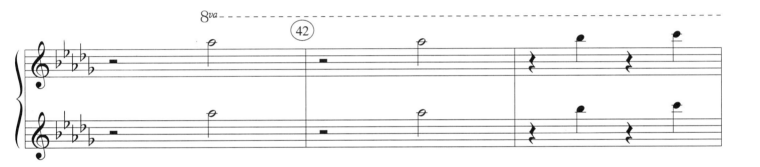
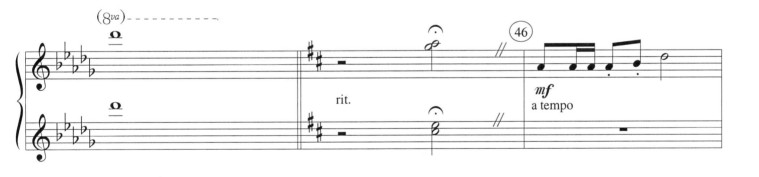

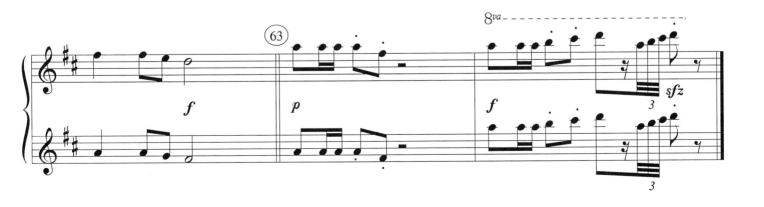

He Lives!

SECONDO

Moderate - Advanced

ALFRED H. ACKLEY
Arranged by Marilynn Ham

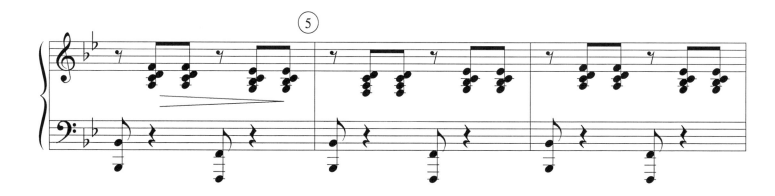

He Lives!

PRIMO

Easy - Moderate

ALFRED H. ACKLEY
Arranged by Mariynn Ham

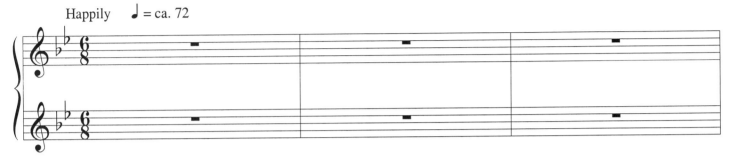

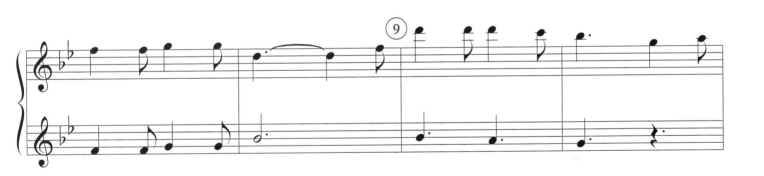

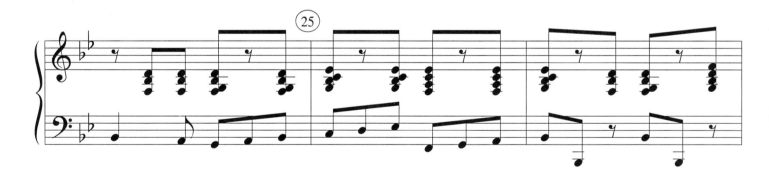

Ped. ad lib.

Change places! (37) (Easy - Moderate player)
Much slower

Mary's Baby (Christmas Medley)

SECONDO

Moderate - Advanced

Arranged by Marilynn Ham

"Mary Had a Little Lamb" (Traditional)

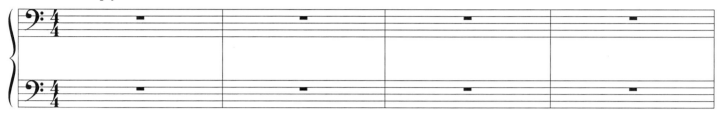

"Mary Had a Baby" (Spiritual)

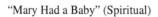

Mary's Baby (Christmas Medley)

PRIMO

Easy - Moderate

Arranged by Marilynn Ham

"Mary Had a Little Lamb" (Traditional)

"Mary Had a Baby" (Spiritual)

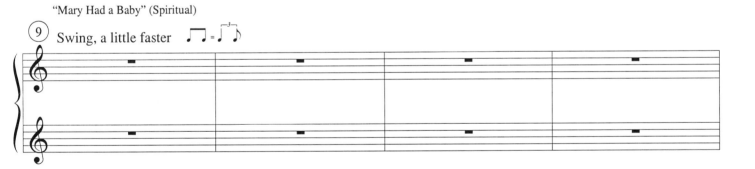

"The Virgin Mary Had a Baby Boy" (Traditional)

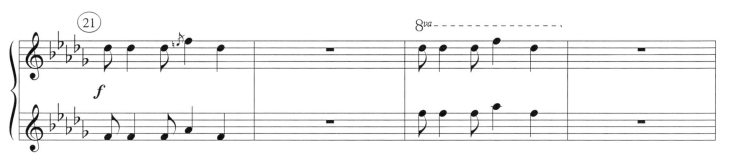

"The Virgin Mary Had a Baby Boy" (Traditional)

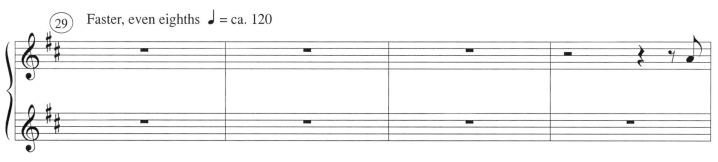

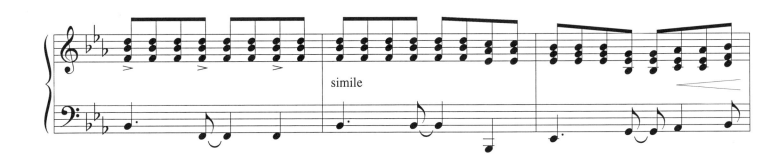

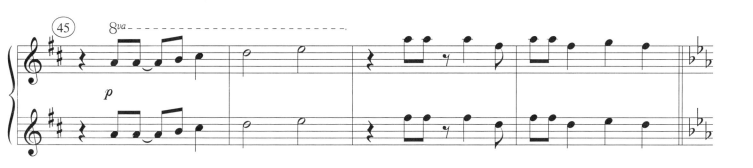

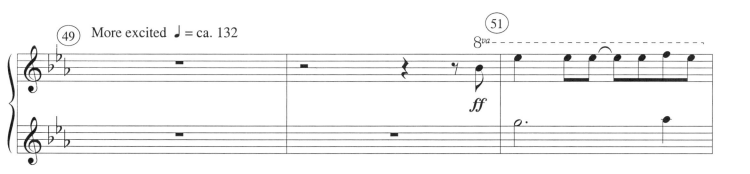

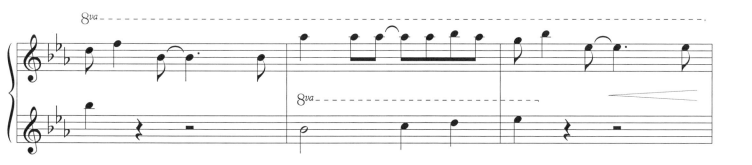

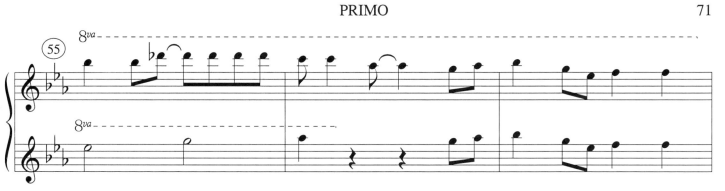

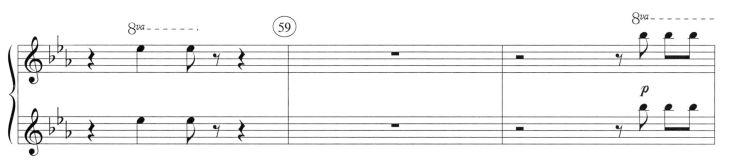

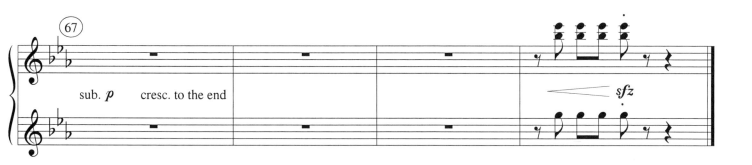